It's Worth the Ride to
the Wayside

Celebrating **100** Years with
Anniversary Ale, Yankee Cooking,
and Ice Cream!

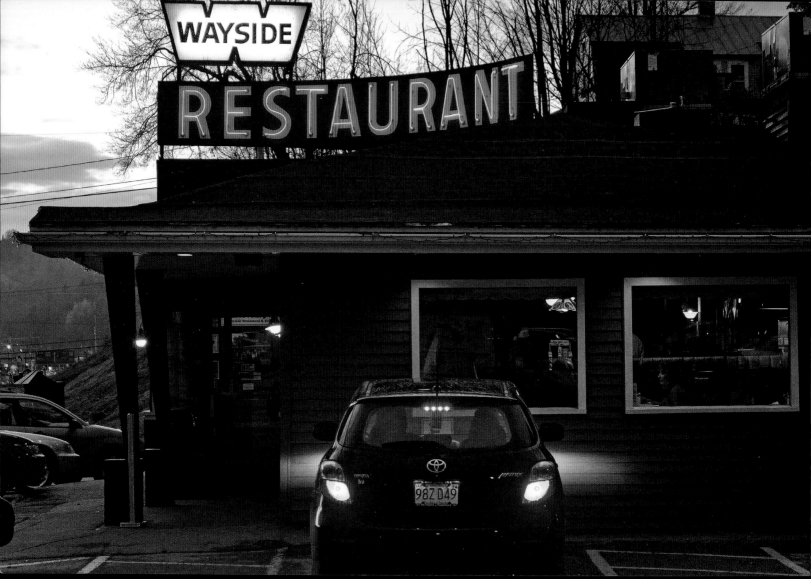

A WARM WAYSIDE WELCOME

"Thank you for coming." Folks in the food-service industry can't say that enough. The dining public today has many choices, so you better make darn sure you show them some love when they walk through your front door. Chances are they've driven past many dining establishments to get to yours.

It is a privilege to be affiliated with the Wayside. Whether you're an employee or a customer, this place is very special. For any business, let alone a restaurant, to make it 100 years is quite amazing.

Wow, 100 years is a long time. That's 2,600 fortnights, 25 Olympiads, 20 lustrums, 10 decades, over 6 indictions, 5 scores, 2 jubilees, and 1/10 of a millennium!

—A Calculating Kid

According to cookbook author Rick Browne in his 2013 book *A Century of Restaurants*, he was only able to identify 240 century-old restaurants across America. The National Restaurant Association reports that there are over one million restaurant locations in the United States. Do the math. Only a small fraction of one percent have made it to the 100-year mark!

The Wayside has prevailed through the Great Depression, World War II, the Vietnam War, and most recently, the Great Recession (2007–2009), just to name a few. Day in and day out, valued employees show up to do their jobs at the Wayside. They know they are appreciated by their coworkers, management, owners, and the community.

It's clearly been an interesting and well-earned ride for everyone that's ever been associated with the Wayside. Now, it's time for you to read on and enjoy learning more about the now "historic" Wayside!

THE FIRST FIFTY YEARS

Imagine what life was like back in 1918. America was in the midst of World War I. It was a year when color movies were invented, Woodrow Wilson was President, and the cost of a first-class postage stamp was 3 cents. Many famous people, including Nelson Mandela, Paul Harvey, Ella Fitzgerald, Billy Graham, Betty Ford, and Howard Cosell, were born that year.

> *I can remember when the 1927 flood stopped the trolley from running, but not your business. I come here to eat whenever I can, mostly at dinner time.*
> —Raymond Witham

During July of that year, a lady by the name of Effie Ballou decided to open a roadside eatery at the foot of the hill below her house. She used to make pies and donuts at the house and bring them down to the Wayside. It was only a small lunchtime establishment back then.

Given the high failure rate of startup food-service businesses, it's probably a good thing Effie didn't know that the Spanish Flu epidemic was about to hit Vermont in August. The flu took more lives in the United States than did World War I. Over 200 Vermonters, many from neighboring Barre, died, and the State Board of Health banned public meetings until the pandemic subsided.

Effie Ballou (bottom right) and her family

George, and his wife, Vivian. They successfully ran the Wayside until 1966.

A great run by the Wayside's first two families—the Ballous and the Fishs.

The Wayside under the Ballou Family, 1910s–1940s

The Wayside under the Fish Family, 1940s–1960s

Joseph and Amy Fish purchased the Wayside in 1945. Under their watch, the Wayside continued to prosper. Nine years later, they sold the restaurant to their son,

W

OYSTER STEW

1	quart standard oysters
1	pound butter
3	cups whole milk
1	cup heavy cream
1/2	teaspoon salt
1/2	teaspoon pepper

Sauté the oysters in the butter in a large skillet until the edges curl. Add the milk, cream, salt and pepper. Cook over low heat until heated through; do not boil. Ladle into soup bowls. Serve with oyster crackers.

Serves 4

Yankee Cooking at its Best Since 1918

A large assortment of alls, shorts, shirts, etc. Little Dry Goods store, 329 North Main.—adv.

FRIDAY, JUNE 30, 1939. open all day Tuesday.—adv.

Busine
Boys' togs for Toggery shop.—a Friday and Sa and colored hats. street.—adv.
Shareholders i tive, Building, S ciation are notifi should be paid c day, July 5.—ad Dancing every Point Comfort, (EST). Music i by Club Royale ments. Big holi adv.

WAYSIDE -- SUNDAY DINNER 75c

ON MONTPELIER ROAD

Grapefruit Cocktail or Chicken Soup
Roast Native Chicken, Dressing
Fresh Vegetable Salad, String Beans, Mashed Potatoes
Apple, Strawberry, Butterscotch Pies
Strawberry Short Cake, Jello, Ice Cream
Tea Coffee or Milk.

"Try Our Fried Clams."

Ge
FIRE
Sale Sta

THE MOST RECENT FIFTY YEARS

The third and current family to operate the Wayside unites two generations of the Galfetti family. Collectively, Eugene and Harriet Galfetti and Brian and Karen Galfetti Zecchinelli have been running this growing business for over fifty years!

Change was in the air when the Galfettis became proprietors of the Wayside. They had just sold out their share of the seasonally popular Twin's A&W snack bar about a mile up the road. With three kids, including their daughter and future owner, Karen, and two more yet to come, Eugene and Harriet wanted to be involved in a year-round operation.

Karen and her father, Eugene Galfetti

It didn't take them long to realize that the Wayside had tremendous potential. When the line to get in the door stretched around the corner of the building, it was time for another addition. Over the course of about

I'm always fond of your breakfasts. I especially enjoy your lobster (salad) roll for lunch...I'm amazed at how consistently good the Wayside food has been over the years with (3) different owners...
—George Anderson

thirty years, Eugene orchestrated seven additions and countless renovations, many without even closing the restaurant. He didn't want loyal customers to get used to drinking their coffee elsewhere.

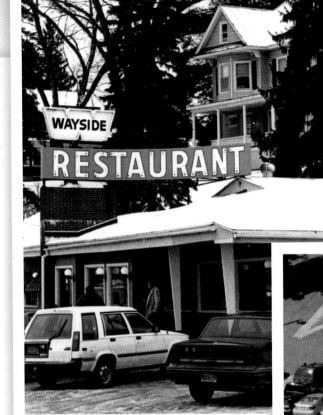

1960s–1980s

1990s–2010s

Today, Eugene and Harriet's daughter Karen and son-in-law Brian enjoy running the business. They both give full credit to Karen's parents for making the place what it is today. There are no plans for expansion of the restaurant. Karen and Brian both acknowledge that the Wayside is the perfect size. They've seen some restaurants get too big and fail. Their hope is that the Wayside will be around for generations to come.

W

FRENCH ONION SOUP

5	*pounds onions, julienned*
2	*tablespoons butter*
2	*tablespoons sugar*
2	*tablespoons salt*
1	*teaspoon black pepper*
1	*tablespoon chopped garlic*
1/2	*cup red wine*
3	*beef bouillon cubes*
2	*quarts beef broth*
2	*quarts chicken broth*
10	*slices bread, toasted*
10	*slices Cheddar cheese*

Combine the onions, butter, sugar, salt, pepper, garlic, wine and bouillon cubes in a stockpot. Simmer for 20 minutes. Stir in the beef broth and chicken broth. Simmer for 1 hour. Ladle into 10 ovenproof soup bowls or crocks. Trim the toast to fit in the bowls. Top each bowl with toast and Cheddar cheese. Broil for 2 minutes or until the cheese is melted and browned.

Serves 10

Yankee Cooking at its Best Since 1918

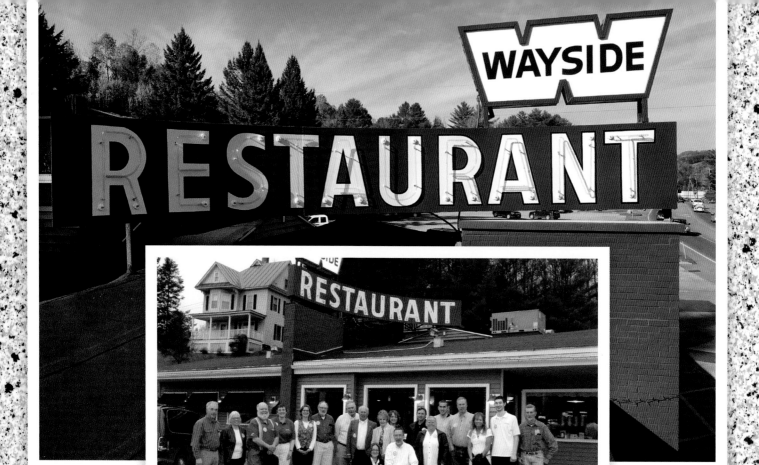

Local Farmers, Foragers, Fishermen, and Friends

THE WAYSIDE TODAY

Some people still call the Wayside a diner, but most call it a restaurant. However you describe the building or fare, to most visitors, it's like coming home. For so many, gone are the days when families would sit around the Sunday table each week with several generations of family and friends, enjoying good homemade comfort food—a setting where people learned about your life and gave encouragement and support.

I would come down often with Mildred (my wife) and besides the good food, we used to see many friends and neighbors from South Barre and surrounding areas.
—Albert Hutchins

That sense of community is what customers find at the Wayside.

On any given day and at any given time, you will find people from all walks of life and all ages, coming together to enjoy the feeling only a family can provide. You might find a retired school teacher giving praise to the youngster reading a book while waiting for his or her meal or an elderly patron playing peek-a-boo with the baby in the highchair at the next table. Then, you have the young couple stopping to ask the plumber or electrician for some lunchtime advice.

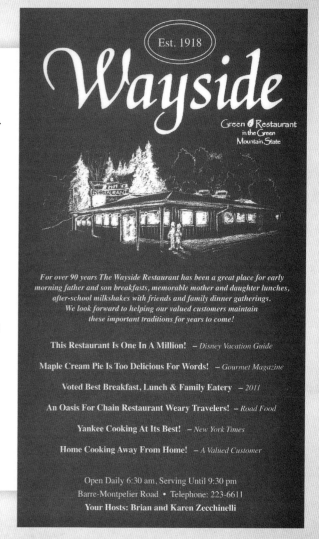

CRANBERRY HAM LOAF

2	*pounds finely chopped ham*	1	*cup diced green bell pepper*
1	*pound ground mild pork sausage*	1	*cup milk*
3	*cups bread crumbs*	2	*medium eggs, beaten*
2	*cups diced onions*		*Cranberry Glaze*

Combine the ham, sausage, bread crumbs, onions, bell pepper, milk and eggs in a large bowl and mix well. Shape into a loaf.

Place the loaf in a 9×12-inch baking pan. Bake at 350 degrees for 1 hour. Pour off the pan drippings carefully. Spread with the Cranberry Glaze. Bake for 20 minutes.

CRANBERRY GLAZE

1	*(16-ounce) can whole cranberry sauce*	1/4	*cup water*
		1	*tablespoon corn syrup*

Combine the cranberry sauce, water and corn syrup in a small saucepan. Bring to a boil. Reduce the heat and simmer for 5 minutes or until thickened.

Serves 10

Yankee Cooking at its Best Since 1918

Whether you are a "regular" or a customer who only gets out to dinner once in a while, you can always count on a friendly smile and a reasonably priced homemade meal. You will also have the opportunity to run into family and friends—old and new—who will ask how you're doing and give you that sense of belonging that you had sitting around Grandma's table, oh, so long ago.

BREAKFAST ALL DAY

The baker and the breakfast cook both arrive to work at 5:30 a.m. The breakfast cook fires up all the grills and fryolators and finalizes and prepares the daily breakfast specials, all before the Wayside opens to the general public at 6:30 a.m.

In the meantime, the baker is busy right out of the gate, preparing homemade muffins and old-fashioned buttermilk donuts from scratch. Early-bird patrons are treated to complimentary donut holes—plain or cinnamon-sugared. The servers out front are getting busy, too. They are brewing the coffee, tying up loose ends from the night before, and getting ready for the busy day ahead.

Vermont farm-fresh eggs, dairy, meats, and produce are brought in by valued suppliers throughout the morning. The breakfast cooks continue to do their own thing, flipping eggs, folding omelets, and mass-producing a grill full of buttermilk pancakes and French toast made from their homemade bread—soon to be topped with real Vermont maple syrup!

My favorite meal is breakfast and the coffee is superb! If I'm lucky there will be fruit muffins and super homemade donuts still available.

—Ruth Guild

The servers out front are now busy taking care of the "regulars" and those just looking for a quick and nutritious breakfast. Upon arrival, many customers have their coffee already poured and waiting for them at their favorite stool, booth, or table. Oftentimes, short stories are exchanged amongst the servers and guests. Over the years, you learn a lot about each others' families, hobbies, and habits.

W

HOMEMADE QUICHE

3	medium eggs
1	cup milk
1	cup heavy cream
1/2	teaspoon salt
1/4	teaspoon pepper
12	ounces shredded Swiss cheese
12	ounces shredded Cheddar cheese
1 1/2	cups thinly sliced ham, chopped
1 1/2	cups diced fresh tomatoes
1	cup finely diced onion
2	pie shells

Combine the eggs, milk, cream, salt and pepper in a bowl and mix well. Divide the Swiss cheese, Cheddar cheese, ham, tomatoes and onion evenly between the 2 pie shells. Pour half the egg mixture into each shell. Place the filled pie shells on a baking sheet to catch any spills. Bake at 350 degrees for 1 hour and 15 minutes or until golden brown. Let stand for 15 minutes before cutting.

Serves 10

Yankee Cooking at its Best Since 1918

red flan·nel hash (red flan′ əl hash)
Hash that is served a day or so after families enjoy a traditional New England Boiled Dinner. All the corned beef, cabbage, potatoes, carrots, turnips, and (red) beets are ground into this mouthwatering hash.

Lunch Hour

In preparation for lunch, the day chef prepares two homemade soups daily. Customers often have a difficult time deciding which soup to choose (order a cup of each; problem solved).

Daily lunch and dinner menus are finalized and prepared during the morning. By 11 a.m., all four specials (sometimes more) are ready to go. The Today's Special is the same week after week, year after year. Monday is Roast Beef, Tuesday is Baked Ham, Wednesday is Chicken Pie, Thursday is Roast Pork, Friday is Baked Haddock, Saturday is Pot Roast, and Sunday is Roast Turkey. Other daily specials allow the chefs to express their creativity with classic casseroles, salads, chicken, pork chops, and more.

At high noon, the focus shifts from preparing and cooking food to promptly serving the customers. Another cook is

> *The Wayside Restaurant has always furnished a good meal, for a decent price. Whatever soup is on special, it's all excellent.*
>
> —William Chaloux

Bakery Fresh Sandwiches

McKenzie Hot Dog	2.95
Grilled Cheese (GF)	2.95
Turkey or Tuna Salad (GF)	3.95
Sliced Baked Ham (GF)	3.95
Sliced Roast Turkey (GF)	3.95
Sliced Roast Beef (GF)	3.95
BLT with Mayo (GF)	3.95
Veggie Burger On a Bun	4.50
Western (ham, onion & egg) (GF)	4.50
Grilled Ham & Cheese (GF)	4.95
Hot Turkey With Gravy	4.95
Hot Roast Beef With Gravy	4.95
Chicken Breast Fillet On a Bun	4.95
Clam Strip Roll	4.95
Fresh Haddock Fishwich On a Bun	4.95
Lobster Salad Roll	5.95

Fish

Haddock Fish & Chips......8.95

Chunks of Fried Haddock

Served with Hand-Cut Fries

Burger

Quarter Pound Burger	3.95
Wayside Double Whammy	5.95
(Two patties, Lettuce & Tomato)	

Open Hot Burgers With Gravy........5.95

Wayside Club with Ham or Turkey ...5.95

(Upgrade To A "Deluxe" With Your Choice Of Two Sides For Only......3.95)

(Upgrade One Side To Sweet Potato Tots, Onion Rings Or Tossed Salad Add 1.50)

Featuring Homemade Bread: White, Honey-Wheat or Rye

 ## Spring Mix Salads

Featured Homemade Dressings

Maple Balsamic Vinaigrette, Blue Cheese, Buttermilk Ranch

Featured Gluten Free Dressings: Light Italian, Honey-Dijon, 1000 Island, Caesar

Joyce's Veggie Plate: (any three side dishes)......6.50

Harriet's Salad with Turkey, Tuna or Lobster Salad (+1.50) (GF)......7.50

Chef's Salad (Choice of Two: Ham, Turkey, Swiss or Cheddar) (GF)......8.50

Chicken Breast Salad......9.50

(Unseasoned, Montreal, Lemon-Pepper, B-B-Q (GF) or Teriyaki)

Steak Tip Salad......10.50

All salads above are served on a bed of spring mix salad, topped with sliced garden veggies and hard-boiled egg, garnished with olives and a carrot curl, includes roll.

W

SHEPHERD'S PIE

2	pounds ground beef
2	medium onions, finely diced
1	beef bouillon cube
1	teaspoon salt
1	(15-ounce) can cream-style corn
1	(15-ounce) can whole kernel corn
8	cups mashed potatoes

Combine the ground beef, onions, bouillon cube and salt in a skillet. Cook until the ground beef is browned, stirring to crumble; drain.

Layer the ground beef mixture (bottom layer), cream-style corn, whole kernel corn (middle layer) and mashed potatoes (top layer) in a 9×13-inch baking dish. Garnish with paprika. Bake at 350 degrees for 40 minutes or until golden brown.

Serves 16

Yankee Cooking at its Best Since 1918

brought onto the serving line to make sure customers, including those on a short lunch hour, are all served in a timely fashion.

Once the dust settles and all the midday lunch customers are satisfied, there is a changing of the guard in the kitchen. Between 1:30 p.m. and 2:30 p.m., the day crew transitions to the night crew. The lunch menu continues until 4:00 p.m., when the popular Soup & Sandwich special

will change to a more substantial cooked-to-order seafood or steak entrée.

DINNER BELL RINGS

If you get to the Wayside early for dinner, there's a good chance you will get to enjoy some Garlic Toasties before they run out. The number of Parker House rolls left over from the previous day determines the supply. Yesterday's rolls are put through the bread slicer, brushed with butter, seasoned with garlic salt, and baked—a taste sensation.

Yes, the Wayside has a full bar, tended by your server. Don't go getting fancy on them, but the bar features the basic "well" liquors plus many premium spirits. Bloody Marys, Margaritas, and Champagne Mimosas (on the weekends) are quite popular. If you like draft beer, try the Wayside's locally brewed Anniversary Ale. Cheers!

My late husband was a state senator for 22 years and we traveled the Barre-Montpelier Road almost daily and the Wayside was our favorite "supper" stop! Your daily menu always has great chicken and fish entrées—fabulous pies and sundaes. Harriet's salad is a special for me!

—Ruth Smith

With a larger demand for broiled seafood, chicken, and steaks during the evening, the broiler cooks get to strut their stuff a little more. They feature both Whole Belly Clams and fresh Clam Strips. Customers typically love one or the other, not both. Seafood is delivered two times a week from Boston. It's the Wayside's version of boat-to-table dining.

After the dinner rush, it's time to start cleaning up and getting ready for the next day. Cooks and servers take great pride in pulling off another successful day at the Wayside. They also realize that you cannot rest on your laurels in the restaurant business. You're only as good as your last meal.

Sunday Nite

Prime RIB

Central Vermonter's First Choice Any Season!

DINNER SPECIALS

Served 11 a.m. to 9:30 p.m. Every Week!

APPETIZERS: Soup or Juice

Monday — Roast Beef
Tuesday — Baked Ham
Wednesday — Chicken Pie
Thursday — Roast Pork
Friday — Baked Haddock
Saturday — Pot Roast
Sunday — Roast Turkey

All include potato, vegetable, roll & butter

**All Roasted Meats are
Hand Carved to Order.**

W

LONDON BROIL

1/2	cup soy sauce
2	tablespoons vegetable oil
2	tablespoons red wine vinegar
1	tablespoon local honey
1	teaspoon garlic salt
2	pounds flank steak (about 1 inch thick)

Combine the soy sauce, vegetable oil, vinegar, honey and garlic salt in a large dish and mix well. Add the steak. Marinate, covered, in the refrigerator for 4 to 6 hours or overnight, turning occasionally.

Place the steak on a rack in a broiler pan. Broil 5 inches from the heat source for 3 to 5 minutes per side for medium-rare. Remove to a serving platter. Slice across the grain and serve.

Serves 4

Yankee Cooking at its Best Since 1918

COUNTER INTELLIGENCE

In the early days, the counter was small, to fit the size of the building. It evolved into a long high-top counter with many stools. In the 1960s, that counter was dismantled and two horseshoe-shaped counters were installed to encourage more friendly back-and-forth conversation. Today, there remains a single horseshoe-shaped counter that comfortably seats twelve of the Wayside's finest guests.

One time an older friend of mine invited me to go to the Wayside after skiing for the "best ever" French fries—they were right. Then and now! Everything is good—I can depend on it!

—Claire Couture

It has been observed by newcomers to the counter or folks sitting nearby that they don't need to buy a newspaper. All the problems of the world are analyzed, debated, and solved at the counter right then and there.

Each day, there are three unofficial meeting times—the crack of dawn, 9 a.m. plus or minus, and mid-afternoon coffee break.

Someone along the way coined the term "Counter Intelligence" (not counterintelligence) for this distinguished group of men and

W LOVE POTION COCKTAIL

2   *parts coconut rum*
1   *part cranberry juice*
1   *part orange juice*

Fill a hurricane glass or red plastic cup with ice. Add the coconut rum, cranberry juice and orange juice and stir. Garnish with a maraschino cherry and enjoy!

Serves 1

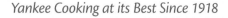

Yankee Cooking at its Best Since 1918

women who frequent the counter daily. That's when the Wayside decided to print up some special T-shirts just for them and eventually for others. The design of the shirt was expertly proofed and sent to press. When the 144 shirts arrived "intelligence" was misspelled (see photo below). It's like it was meant to be, a tongue-in-cheek mistake. They still sold like crazy.

The T-shirts were worn for years to come, like a badge of honor.

RISE AND SHINE BAKERY

The Wayside Bakery is certainly a feather in the Wayside Restaurant's cap. A team of bakers works seven days a week from 5:30 a.m. to 1:30 p.m.—more if needed. From morning until night, Wayside customers enjoy baked goods made from scratch with the exception of only four items: New England–style hot dog buns, English muffins, bagels, and gluten-free bread.

Once the muffins and donuts are finished in the morning, bakers promptly start making bread, puddings, pies, cakes, squares, and, of course, Parker House rolls. Speaking of rolls, did you know that a Wayside hamburger bun is made from the same Parker House roll recipe, proofed, and baked? That explains why Wayside burgers taste so good!

Leave your baking to the Wayside. "Just like Grandma's," folks have said. The bakery features 10-inch deep-dish pies. Customer favorites include maple cream, pecan, chocolate cream, lemon meringue, pumpkin, custard, and all their fruit pies (raspberry, apple, and blueberry, to name a few). Around the Christmas and New Year's holidays, their Canadian tourtière (pork pie), served with homemade pork gravy, is a top seller.

While every holiday throughout the year is busy in the bakery, Thanksgiving takes the cake. Orders start coming in one month in advance. Bakers work around the clock to make over 200 pies and 500 dozen rolls for pickup during Thanksgiving week. If you'd like to see how a Wayside apple pie is made, go to waysiderestaurant.com and view Videos/The Pie Tour. You're sure to order a slice of pie on your next visit or order a whole pie for a special occasion, like your birthday!

Vermont Maple Cream Pies

LIVE FREE OR PIE
WAYSIDE
Vermont SINCE 1918

GINGER "NO-SNAP" HOLIDAY COOKIES

2	cups sugar	2	teaspoons baking soda
1 1/2	cups shortening		
4	eggs	2	teaspoons ground cinnamon
1/2	cup molasses		
2	teaspoons vanilla extract	2	teaspoons ground ginger
4 1/2	cups all-purpose flour	Sugar for sprinkling	

Combine the sugar, shortening, eggs, molasses and vanilla extract in a large bowl and mix well.

Sift the flour, baking soda, cinnamon and ginger into a bowl. Add the flour mixture to the sugar mixture and mix well. Refrigerate for 30 minutes.

Shape the dough into 1 1/2-inch balls, flattening to 1/2 inch thick. Sprinkle with sugar. Arrange on baking sheets. Bake at 350 degrees for 10 minutes.

May pat the dough 1/2 inch thick on a floured surface, cut with holiday cookie cutters and decorate as desired.

Serves 24

Yankee Cooking at its Best Since 1918

CREAMERY FRESH

"How can we make the Wayside better?" That's a question the owners, managers, and employees routinely ask themselves. They know better than to make any wholesale changes (you don't want to mess with success), but a few tweaks here and there will keep the Wayside—fresh.

Ownership and staff have always taken great pride in serving home-cooked meals, starting with the homemade soups all the way to the slice of homemade pie for dessert. Years ago, if you wanted apple pie à la mode, you got a scoop of store-bought vanilla ice cream. STOP. "Why don't we make our own ice cream?" the Wayside asked. That's when the Wayside Creamery was born.

I was a child age 4 in 1927, my first introduction to the Wayside. My grandpa brought me down for ice cream. I have been eating at the Wayside for 81 years and I believe this is the oldest continuous business on the Barre/Montpelier Road.
—Dorothy Cayia

There began the journey to make the most delicious vanilla ice cream possible that goes best with apple pie. For months, the creamery team experimented with its new ice cream machine.

W

APPLE CRISP

8   cups sliced Granny Smith apples
1   tablespoon lemon juice
2   cups all-purpose flour, divided
1½   cups sugar
1   teaspoon ground cinnamon
1½   cups rolled oats
1½   cups packed brown sugar
¾   cup butter, melted

Place the apples in a large bowl and sprinkle with the lemon juice, tossing to coat. Add ½ cup flour, sugar and cinnamon and toss to coat. Spoon into a 9×13-inch baking pan.

Combine the oats, remaining 1½ cups flour, brown sugar and butter in a bowl and mix well. Sprinkle over the apple mixture. Bake at 350 degrees for 1 hour.

This dessert tastes best when served à la mode.

Serves 12

Yankee Cooking at its Best Since 1918

Employees lined up to take the factory seconds home. They were still better than most ice creams found in the local stores.

Once the vanilla ice cream recipe was perfected (now called Signature Vanilla), it was time to move on to other flavors. Their "smooth" flavor spectrum has evolved to include chocolate, cranberry, Vermont maple, blue raspberry, pomegranate, black raspberry, root beer, orange, lemonade, mango, strawberry, and coffee, to name a few. As for the future? Change can be good.

THE RED SOX FINALLY WIN!

For years, the Wayside had a 9×9-foot banner displayed at the local Mountaineers baseball field that said, "Wayside Restaurant, Established 1918, The Last Year the Red Sox Won the World Series." Remember, Babe Ruth was a member of that championship team.

To make matters worse, ownership was starting to run ads proclaiming that the Wayside would roll the prices back to 1918 if the Red Sox ever won the World Series! After World Series losses in 1946, 1967, 1975, and 1986, customers acknowledged that this was a shrewd business move, and the Wayside would never have to pay up.

Much to everyone's surprise and the owners' true happiness, the Red Sox won the

World Series in 2004 after an 86-year drought! Now, it was time to have a party for the ages. The stage was set. Red Sox balloons were floating throughout the restaurant, and all of the employees were wearing their favorite Red Sox gear.

I first ate at the Wayside in 1948. We sat on stools then. My cousin and I ate from a large bowl of fried clams. They were very good and we over ate.
—Beverly Knapp

One of that day's customers had a rubbing of her father's tombstone with her because she wanted him to be at the party in spirit. "Take Me Out to the Ball Game" was sung by the patrons every hour on the hour. It was a day that all of the employees and 3,000 plus customers will never forget!

1918 Pennant

2004 Pennant

As for the banner, it's been laid to rest. Before being put into storage, it was brought to one last Mountaineers baseball game and signed by that evening's special guest: Julia "Ruth" Stevens, the Babe's daughter. The "curse" was officially over.

Do You Have Moxie?

It took a ride to Plymouth Notch, Vermont, home of America's thirtieth president, to realize that Moxie belonged on the menu. Moxie was Calvin Coolidge's favorite soft drink.

I was just a kid when I first came. I sat in the car between Mom and Dad (no seat belts) and it was a treat in those days to go to a "restaurant" to eat. We always loved the Wayside and still do.

—Andrea Rancourt

The Wayside has always taken great pride in serving local New England favorites. Longstanding customers enjoy the New England Boiled Dinner, Beans & Franks (a Saturday night staple in old-time Vermont households), Salt Pork and Milk Gravy, Fried Pickled Honeycomb Tripe, Grape-Nut Custard Pudding, and, of course, Parker House rolls. Moxie seemed like the perfect beverage to wash everything down.

Back in the day, local Red Sox hero and future Hall of Famer Ted Williams proclaimed, "Make

Mine MOXIE" in print ads, on posters, and on embossed tin signs and magnets. If the "Splendid Splinter" thought we should all drink Moxie, it had to be good!

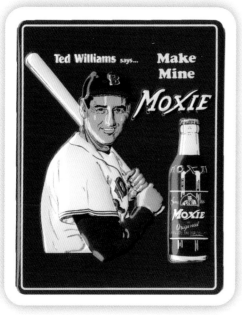

W

MOXIE CHILI

2	(12-ounce) bottles Moxie soda	1	(16-ounce) can diced tomatoes
2	pounds ground beef	1	(16-ounce) can red kidney beans, drained
1	cup chopped onion	1	(8-ounce) can tomato sauce
3/4	cup chopped green bell pepper	2	teaspoons taco seasoning mix
1	teaspoon chopped garlic	2	teaspoons salt
		1	teaspoon pepper

Pour the Moxie into a saucepan. Bring to a rolling boil. Boil for 24 minutes or until reduced by three-fourths.

Brown the ground beef with the onion, bell pepper and garlic in a stockpot, stirring until crumbly; drain. Stir in the reduced Moxie, undrained tomatoes, kidney beans, tomato sauce, taco seasoning mix, salt and pepper. Simmer, covered, for 20 minutes. Ladle into soup bowls.

Feel free to enter this in your local chili cook-off!

Serves 12

Yankee Cooking at its Best Since 1918

𝒲

Moxie Barbecue Sauce

2	(12-ounce) bottles Moxie soda
3	cups ketchup
1/4	cup Worcestershire sauce
2	tablespoons red wine vinegar
1	tablespoon salt
1	teaspoon pepper

Pour the Moxie into a saucepan. Bring to a rolling boil. Boil for 24 minutes or until reduced by three-fourths. Let stand to cool.

Add the ketchup, Worcestershire sauce, red wine vinegar, salt and pepper to the reduced Moxie and mix well.

Coat chicken, pork or beef generously with the sauce for a little extra giddyup on your grill!

Makes 1 quart

Yankee Cooking at its Best Since 1918

There is a loyal following of Moxie customers at the Wayside. People either love it or hate it. Those that enjoy it are encouraged to join the New England Moxie Congress, a fraternal organization of Moxie-minded people.

In 2007, Coca-Cola of Northern New England (CCNNE) purchased the rights to the Moxie brand. Go to drinkmoxie.com and select Moxology, Products, Events, and History for more information. There's even a Moxie parade every summer!

WINTER WONDERLAND

'Tis the season for hats, scarves, coats, mittens, and tasty Wayside comfort food. There's even a cozy gas stove in the back room—the perfect place for fireside chats over coffee or for memorable family gatherings.

While some say that Vermont has nine months of winter and three months of bad skiing, others will tell you there are two seasons in Vermont—winter and the fourth of July. Regardless, once the ponds and lakes freeze over, neighboring ice fishermen start bringing local fresh perch to the Wayside.

Favorite food to have anytime—local perch.

—Irene Eastman

Customers claim that winter-caught perch are far superior to summer-caught perch. The fishermen bring in the perch fully dressed and almost ready to go. The kitchen crew only has to trim off the ribs and divide the fish into 1/2-pound portions. The experienced fry cooks hand-batter and deep-fry the perch to order.

The golden brown perch are then devoured by customers from near

and far. Be sure to watch an old "perch pro" at the table next to you so you can refine your technique of peeling the delicious perch fillets off the backbone. Spritz them with some lemon juice, salt and pepper to taste, or simply enjoy them with the Wayside's homemade tartar sauce.

SUPER BOWL BRATS

10   *precooked bratwurst*
27   *ounces drained sauerkraut*
Favorite beer

Brown the bratwurst in a skillet over medium-high heat.

Spoon half the sauerkraut into a 9×12-inch baking pan. Arrange the bratwurst over the sauerkraut. Top with the remaining sauerkraut. Pour enough beer over the top to cover the sauerkraut. Bake, tightly covered with foil, at 300 degrees for 3 hours, adding additional beer as needed to keep the sauerkraut covered.

Your guests can cut the brats with a fork; no knife is required.

Serves 6

Yankee Cooking at its Best Since 1918

39

Now Serving:
FIDDLEHEADS

Spring Has Sprung

If you look at a calendar, it would appear that spring follows winter. However, ask any Vermonter, and they will tell you that Mud Season follows winter. As the snow begins to melt, April showers turn miles of rural dirt roads into a muddy mess.

The good news is that along the nearby streams, brooks, and rivers, fiddlehead ferns begin to sprout up. Experienced foragers begin to pick the "fiddles" one by one. They are careful not to trample down the beds so these precious areas can continue to produce wonderful fiddleheads for years to come.

The fiddleheads—already cleaned and ready to cook—are delivered to the restaurant through the back door. Customers flock to the Wayside to get their first taste of spring. Steamed fiddleheads are on the menu every day as a side dish as long as they last.

> *My fond memory was taking my date to the Wayside the night I graduated in June 1939. That way I didn't have to spend a lot of money to get something good to eat. I always look for fiddleheads in the spring!*
> —Cecil "Pete" Tucker

W

KENTUCKY DERBY PUDDING

1	*pound sugar*
2	*cups dark corn syrup*
2	*cups beaten eggs*
1	*cup butter, melted*
1	*cup semisweet chocolate chips*
1	*cup crushed pecans*
3	*ounces bourbon*

Combine the sugar, corn syrup, eggs, butter, chocolate chips, pecans and bourbon in a bowl and mix well.

Pour the mixture into a 9×12-inch baking pan. Bake at 350 degrees for 1 hour and 15 minutes, stirring twice.

Serves 10

Yankee Cooking at its Best Since 1918

They can be enjoyed plain or with butter, salt, and pepper. Some people ask for a cruet of red wine vinegar to season their fiddleheads.

On days when they have an abundance of fiddleheads, the chefs like to prepare Creamy Fiddlehead Soup and Homemade Fiddlehead Quiche. If you're lucky, the weekend breakfast cooks will feature a Fiddlehead and Cheddar Cheese Omelet as a special. The culinary sky is the limit for this green, nutty-flavored Vermont delicacy.

SUMMER SPLENDOR

Summer is the favorite season for most Wayside employees. June is a great month because that's when the strawberries begin to ripen. If the managers forget to put it on the menu, customers remind the servers: "we want shortcake." The bakers quickly get to work and start cutting up strawberries and mixing in just the right amount of sugar. The fresh strawberry topping is served over buttermilk biscuits and garnished with real whipped cream!

"Knee high by the fourth of July." Everyone is keeping an eye on the local corn crop. Before you know it, the phone is ringing, and a local farmer is on the line asking, "Are you ready for some corn?" The answer is always, "Yes."

For the next eight weeks, an amazing relationship unfolds. To achieve maximum freshness, a par level is established of how many ears of corn customers eat each day of the week. From then on, the night manager receives a call from their farmer friend each evening to see how many ears are left—fourteen, five, or none.

I remember coming here nearly every week for lunch with my brother for a long time. We enjoyed your chicken pie and strawberry shortcake in June.

—Patricia Jennings

The next day's par level delivery is adjusted accordingly. The perfect amount of corn is delivered by 9 a.m., shucked by 10 a.m., and on the lunch menu at 11 a.m. You can't get any fresher than that!

Customers young and old eagerly wait for their meal to arrive with a locally picked ear of corn as their side dish.

SERVING FRESH LOCAL CORN

The chefs have determined that corn on the cob this fresh can be eaten raw. However, they do steam the corn for five minutes, just to get the kernels hot, and serve it with butter.

OLD-FASHIONED HAM SALAD

1	pound ground or finely chopped ham
1	teaspoon yellow mustard
3/4	cup mayonnaise
1/2	cup sweet relish

Combine the ham, mustard, mayonnaise and sweet relish in a bowl and mix well.

Serve the ham salad with leaf lettuce on your favorite bread or toast. If counting carbs, put a scoop on a bed of lettuce or your favorite salad greens.

Serves 6

Yankee Cooking at its Best Since 1918

FALL IS IN THE AIR

After the first frost, the leaves on the trees really start to change color. Tourists from all over the world converge on Vermont to see the beautiful foliage—and to EAT. When the leaf peepers come to town in Vermont, it's all hands on deck at the Wayside.

On October 3, 1952, my boyfriend…pulled over to the side of the road…and dropped a ring box in my lap and asked me to marry him. After saying yes, we went to the Wayside for coffee…It's been a part of our life ever since!

—Patricia Towne

People who have grown up in the area can sometimes take the Wayside for granted. It's been around for what seems like forever. Their parents, grandparents, and even great-grandparents have always eaten at the good ole Wayside.

Refreshingly, once the tourists come to town, the staff is reminded daily that "the Wayside is really a special place." Many travelers ask if the Wayside could open a restaurant in their hometown. They rave about the home-cooked food, as well as the friendly and attentive service.

This time of year, everyone seems to really enjoy the winter squash. Between 4,000 and 5,000 pounds of squash are harvested locally and delivered weekly to the restaurant in 50-pound boxes. Upon arrival, the squash is peeled, cut into chunks, steamed, and then mashed with just the right amount of brown sugar, butter, salt, and pepper. Customers really love it.

EAT FRESH FOR HEALTH

W

SQUASH BISQUE

2	pounds diced butternut squash	1	tablepoon salt
		3	quarts chicken or vegetable broth
2	pounds diced potatoes	3/4	cup packed brown sugar
4	ounces diced onions	1	teaspoon ground allspice
4	ounces diced carrots	2	teaspoons ground cinnamon
4	tablespoons butter	2	teaspoons ground nutmeg
1/4	cup cooking sherry	1	cup heavy cream

Combine the squash, potatoes, onions, carrots, butter, sherry and salt in a heavy stockpot. Simmer for 5 minutes, stirring occasionally. Stir in the broth and brown sugar. Cook, covered, for 30 minutes or until the vegetables are tender. Add the allspice, cinnamon and nutmeg and mix well. Pour the mixture into a blender and process until puréed. Return the soup to the stockpot and stir in the heavy cream to finish. Ladle into soup bowls.

Serves 14   *Yankee Cooking at its Best Since 1918*

Wayside Employees' Children—2002

VALUED STAFF TRIBUTE

Hire the best and the brightest. Provide a better-than-competitive wage and keep improving employee benefits. Maintain an atmosphere that is healthy, family-oriented, and committed to one common goal: making sure customers are 110 percent satisfied. All are proven rules for success.

Over the years, the Wayside has done just that—and it shows. It has become a very popular restaurant. Some call it a "Vermont institution." When young high school students apply for their first job, they are reminded (tongue in cheek) that there are four cornerstones in the community. "You absolutely need the hospital, the fire department, the police department, and the Wayside!"

Employees are cross-trained at multiple positions, and even a call-out doesn't disrupt the steady flow of the Wayside. Consequently, employees stick around for a long time, even

I used to work at the Wayside with my son Jeff Virge. I worked there for over 10 years. I had some wonderful people to work with including my son!

—Floy Virge

in an industry that typically has a high turnover rate. With over sixty employees, there are currently six members of the 25-Year Club. The most senior member has over forty years of service. There are nineteen additional employees with ten years of service or more. Former and current employees have encouraged their children and even their grandchildren to work at the Wayside.

Retired Server Aprons Hoisted to the Rafters!

It seems like the busier the restaurant gets, the smoother it runs. Just grab a seat at the counter and take a minute to watch the show in the kitchen and in the dining room. Some make it look so easy—that's called experience.

Three Generations of the Virge Family

CHARLOTTE'S CHICKEN

6	*(6-to 8-ounce) chicken breasts, butterflied*
2	*cups sauerkraut*
1	*cup Thousand Island dressing*
6	*slices Swiss cheese*

Arrange the chicken breasts in a baking dish. Divide the sauerkraut evenly on top of the chicken breasts. Divide the Thousand Island dressing evenly on top of the sauerkraut.

Bake, covered with foil, at 350 degrees for 35 minutes. Top each chicken breast with Swiss cheese. Bake, uncovered, for 10 minutes.

Serves 6

Yankee Cooking at its Best Since 1918

GATHERING ROOM

The Wayside Restaurant Is
ONE IN A MILLION

A Proud Sponsor of the 2006 NECBL Champions
Vermont Mountaineers

Valentine's Day Bandit Strikes Again!

SOCIAL MISSION

The number one goal for the Wayside is to continue to be the hub of this wonderful community—a gathering place where people of all ages and from all walks of life come to experience how we are much more alike than different. The people at the Wayside appreciate how much enjoyment can come from sharing food and the simple things in life, like a caring smile or a "How are you?"

This restaurant strives to be an affordable place for everyone. Keeping the Wayside's prices reasonable is an everyday job. Anyone can raise prices; it's a lot more work to keep them low. Cooks learn all about proper portioning—reducing food costs—and waste. They are very good at making "a silk purse out of a sow's ear," like making a delicious soup out of leftovers.

> *I can remember coming to the Montpelier area when I was dating my husband to be. He took me to dinner before we went to a dance in Williamstown. I was almost 15 years old. Your restaurant is still a favorite. Thanks for keeping the prices reasonable.*
>
> —Elizabeth Witham

WE BELIEVE IN...

Providing our customers with the freshest foods, prepared with care.

We serve FRESH VEGETABLES ALL YEAR 'ROUND...locally grown in season!

Some seasonal specialties on our menu include: Fiddleheads, parsnips, winter squash and even FRESH NATIVE PERCH. While the lakes stay frozen and the fishing's good.

Salt Pork Every Thursday

"We've *never* seen salt pork and gravy served in any other restaurant. It is some trouble to make; and most customers, we reckon, wouldn't recognize salt pork as a fitting main course. But in this part of Vermont, there are enough old-timers around who know just how delicious it can be; and so it is on the menu of the Wayside Restaurant once a week."

THE WAYSIDE'S 1940s MENU

Today's Special 95¢
SOUP or JUICE

....

WHIPPED or FRENCH FRIED POTATOES
................, COLE SLAW or COTTAGE CHEESE
ROLLS & BUTTER   TEA or COFFEE
PUDDING and CREAM

Special 85¢

ROLLS and BUTTER
PUDDING and CREAM

Traveler's Lunch 65¢
CUP OF SOUP

....

SANDWICH WITH FRENCH FRIES
TEA or COFFEE
ICE CREAM

A La Carte

T-Bone Steak	$2.00	Grilled Country Sausage	.90
Tenderloin Steak	1.50	Grilled Liver & Bacon	.90
Club Sirloin Steak	1.35	Fried Haddock (Tartar sauce)	.90
Tenderized Steak	1.15	Fried Scallops (tartar sauce)	1.00
Grilled Pork Chops	1.15	Fried Shrimp (tartar sauce)	1.00
Grilled Ham Steak	1.00	Fried Clams (tartar sauce)	1.00
Breaded Veal Cutlet	1.00	Fried Oysters (tartar sauce)	1.25
Hamburg Steak	.90	Fried Tripe	.90

Fried Half Chicken 1.25
Choice of Potato and Vegetable with above orders
Rolls and Butter

OYSTER STEW (in season) 70¢
POTATO SALAD, FRANKS, or COLD CUTS (in season) 90¢

HOME MADE PIES 20¢		TEA, COFFEE or MILK	10¢
		HOT CHOCOLATE	15¢
APPLE		LARGE MILK	20¢
CUSTARD		LARGE SODA	20¢
PUMPKIN		ICED TEA or COFFEE	15¢

Vermont Meals Tax: .14 to .33 – 1%; .33 to .66 – 2%; .66 to $1.00, Incl. – 3%

THE WAYSIDE'S MENU TODAY

JANUARY 2, 2018   **WELCOME TO THE WAYSIDE**
****
WE'VE UPGRADED OUR NY STRIP TO 2 TENDER FILLETS!
WAYSIDE'S 100TH ANNIVERSARY ALE OR CHAMPAGNE 3.95
* UPGRADE TO A "PREMIUM SPIRIT" FOR ONLY 1.50 *
****
VITAMIN WATER: ACAI-BLUEBERRY-POMEGRANATE 1.75/2.50
REGIONAL BREW: VON TRAPP'S VIENNA AMBER LAGER! 3.95
APPETIZER SPECIAL: ONION BATTERED GREEN BEANS 4.50
SOUP SPECIALS: TOMATO BURGER MAC, CORN CHOWDER
SIDE DISHES: MASHED OR BAKED POTATO, HAND-CUT FRIES,
SWEET POTATO TOTS (+1.50), RICE PILAF, CRANBERRY SAUCE,
COLESLAW, SPRING MIX SALAD (+1.50), COTTAGE CHEESE,
ONION RINGS (+1.50), APPLESAUCE, CHEDDAR GOLDFISH,
POTATO CHIPS, SLICED BEETS, TOMATOES & ZUCCHINI,
QUINOA & KALE SALAD, MANDARIN ORANGES.
****
* TODAY'S SPECIAL *
CHOICE OF SOUP OR JUICE
8.50
MCKENZIE HAM
   VERMONT MAPLE CURED HAM SLOW BAKED WITH MUSTARD
AND BROWN SUGAR, FRUIT SAUCE OPTIONAL.
   CHOICE OF 2 SIDES & FRESH BAKED ROLL
****
* VERMONT SPECIAL *
7.50
TURKEY CASSEROLE
   A BLEND OF TURKEY, GARDEN VEGETABLES AND
EGG NOODLES IN A CREAMY SAUCE SLOW BAKED.
   CHOICE OF 2 SIDES & FRESH ROLL (SOUP ADD 1.50)
****
* TRAVELER'S LUNCH *
CHOICE OF SOUP
6.50
HAM & SWISS
   SLICED HAM, SWISS CHEESE AND LEAF LETTUCE
ON FRESH BAKED BREAD FROM OUR BAKERY.
****
* CHEFS SPECIAL *
8.50
CREAMY DIJON CHICKEN
   A BONELESS CHICKEN BREAST HAND BREADED AND SLOW
BAKED TOPPED WITH A WHITE WINE DIJON CREAM SAUCE.
   CHOICE OF 2 SIDES & FRESH ROLL (ADD SOUP 1.50)
****
* OTHER SPECIALS *
6.50 **OPEN HOT BEEF** ON BREAD, WITH 1 SIDE ABOVE.
10.50 **FRESH LOCAL PERCH**, WITH 2 SIDES & FRESH ROLL.
****
* THANK YOU FOR YOUR PATRONAGE *

WAYSIDE PRIDE

If the pork market is down, plan on seeing ribs or chops on special that month. This is viewed as an opportunity to pass the savings along to the customers, not to make more money. On a weekly basis, chefs take advantage of suppliers' specials to create many delicious meals that don't put a big dent in your wallet.

Don't feel like cooking tonight? Breakfast is now served all day. Lighter meals, including sandwiches, are available during the evening, too. With over 200 items on the menu, there's something for everyone!

CREAMY MAC AND CHEESE

3/4	cup butter	16	ounces Velveeta cheese, cut into 1-inch cubes
1/2	cup all-purpose flour	16	ounces shredded Cheddar cheese
2	teaspoons garlic salt		
1	tablespoon salt	4	ounces shredded Parmesan cheese
1	teaspoon white or black pepper	2	pounds elbow macaroni, cooked al dente
2	teaspoons dry mustard		
2	quarts whole milk		
1	quart heavy cream		

Melt the butter in a large saucepan over medium heat. Stir in the flour, garlic salt, salt, pepper and dry mustard. Remove from the heat. Meanwhile, heat the milk and cream in a double boiler over medium heat.

Add the milk mixture gradually to the flour mixture, whisking constantly. Add the Velveeta cheese, Cheddar cheese and Parmesan cheese. Cook until smooth, stirring frequently.

Divide the macaroni between two 9×13-inch baking pans. Pour the cheese sauce over the macaroni. Bake at 350 degrees for 45 minutes, stirring every 15 minutes.

Serves 16

Yankee Cooking at its Best Since 1918

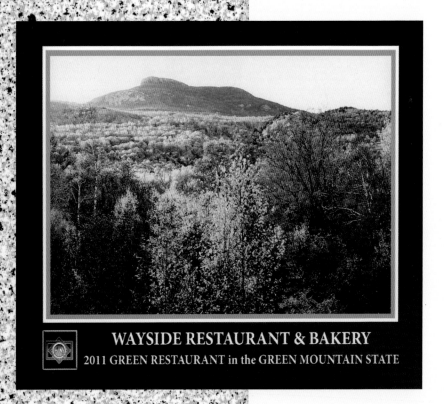

WAYSIDE RESTAURANT & BAKERY
2011 GREEN RESTAURANT in the GREEN MOUNTAIN STATE

GREEN RESTAURANT CERTIFICATION

The Wayside has been going green for a long time, which has been a source of great pride for the entire staff. The Wayside is recognized by the state of Vermont as Montpelier's first Green Restaurant. The staff has adopted the following mission statement: "To be the restaurant industry leader in the areas of waste reduction, energy and water conservation, pollution prevention, and transportation efficiencies for others to follow, including our customers."

A key component to the Wayside's Green Restaurant designation has been its successful composting efforts. The restaurant diverts over 65 tons (that's over 130,000 pounds!) of food scraps annually from the local landfill. Food scraps going to the landfill turn into methane, one of the most powerful greenhouse gases.

At the composting facility, the food scraps are reclaimed into the soil and even provide a good food source for some farm animals. Al Jazeera TV did a feature story

on the Wayside, which can be viewed at waysiderestaurant.com and then select Videos/Wayside Composting.

Does your home or business have a big or small carbon footprint? While all green initiatives are great for the environment, many can save you money in the long term, too.

VERMONT'S 5TH GREEN RESTAURANT

Green Restaurant

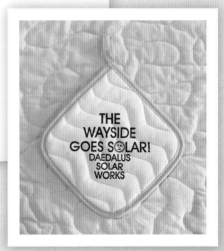

MICROBREW CHEDDAR SOUP

1	pound bacon	2	(12-ounce) bottles
2	medium onions, diced		microbrew
1	red bell pepper, diced	1	teaspoon hot sauce
1	celery heart, diced	16	ounces shredded
6	chicken bouillon cubes		Cheddar cheese
1	cup butter	8	ounces Velveeta cheese,
1/2	cup all-purpose flour		cut into 1/2-inch cubes
2	tablespoons dry mustard	6	ounces shredded
2	quarts water		Parmesan cheese

Arrange the bacon on a rimmed baking sheet. Bake at 350 degrees to desired degree of doneness; drain. Let stand to cool. Crumble the bacon.

Sauté the onions, bell pepper, celery and bouillon cubes in the butter in a stockpot until the vegetables are tender and the bouillon cubes are dissolved. Stir in the flour and dry mustard. Add the water, microbrew and hot sauce gradually, whisking constantly.

Bring to a boil. Add the Cheddar cheese, Velveeta cheese and Parmesan cheese. Cook until the cheese is melted, whisking until smooth. Ladle into soup bowls. Sprinkle with bacon and serve.

Serves 12

Yankee Cooking at its Best Since 1918

Please help us serve you better by filling out the following questionnaire.

Date: _____ Day: _____ Time: _____

How did you hear about us? _____
_____

How often do you come here? _____
_____

What Wayside feature pleases you most? _____
_____

Were you satisfied with the service? _____
_____

Was your server considerate? _____
_____

What changes would you make? _____
_____

Your suggestions for improvement are always welcome. Eugene, Harriet and the rest of the Galfetti family would like to thank you for taking the time to fill out this questionnaire. Your feedback is valuable.

_____
_____
_____
_____
_____
_____
_____

THE NEXT GENERATION

What does the future hold? Chain restaurants are popping up everywhere. Lifestyles are changing, and more and more people are eating out. Chain restaurants play an important role in feeding America. On the flip side of the coin, independent restaurants like the Wayside have the ability to better reflect the heart and soul of their local communities. They provide an oasis for chain-weary locals and travelers.

Bacon, eggs, toast and coffee— roast pork special—roast turkey dinner with all the trimmings— 72 years of "never a bad meal."
—Julian Goodrich

The Wayside continues to get its most productive feedback from its "Penny For Your Thoughts" cards on each table. An old-time Vermonter once commented, "What's this, a penny for my two cents worth?" Another customer who routinely fills out a card with positive feedback refuses to take the penny. She used to come to the Wayside as a kid after church with her grandmother, who used to fill her purse with sugar packets. This nice lady now feels obliged to slowly reimburse the restaurant, one penny at a time!

The current owners hope that independent restaurants across America will continue to work hard to earn their stripes and remain strong. These family-owned and operated restaurants can't do it without continued patronage and feedback. Today, there are so many more ways to provide praise and constructive comments: through e-mails, Facebook, Instagram, Twitter, etc. Restaurateurs can't solve a problem if they don't know about it.

Working together, friends and neighbors can all help make independent restaurants successful in both rural and metropolitan areas—for the next 100 years!

Wayside VERMONT

WAYSIDE RESTAURANT & BAKERY • ESTABLISHED 1918 • YANKEE COOKING AT ITS BEST!

HISTORIC ROUTE 302 • MONTPELIER VT USA

RECIPE INDEX

A few of the recipes below are so rich they should file a tax return! Sure, you can always substitute 2 percent milk for the heavy cream, but why?

METRIC CONVERSION TABLE

UNITED STATES  CANADA

Weights

1 ounce	30 grams
4 ounces	120 grams
8 ounces	225 grams
16 ounces	450 grams

Oven Temperatures

300°F	150°C
325°F	160°C
350°F	180°C
375°F	190°C
400°F	200°C
450°F	230°C

Volume Measurements

1/4 teaspoon		1 mL
1/2 teaspoon		2 mL
1 teaspoon		5 mL
1 tablespoon	3 teaspoons	15 mL
2 tablespoons	1 fluid ounce	30 mL
1/4 cup		60 mL
1/3 cup		75 mL
1/2 cup	4 fluid ounces	125 mL
1 cup	8 fluid ounces	250 mL
2 cups (1 pint)	16 fluid ounces	500 mL
4 cups	1 quart	1 L

Baking Pan Sizes

round	8-inch	20-centimeter (1.2 L)
round	9-inch	23-centimeter (1.5 L)
loaf	5×9 inch	13×23-centimeter (2 L)
square	8-inch	20-centimeter (2 L)
square	9-inch	23×23 centimeters (2.5 L)
rectangle	9×13-inch	23×33 centimeters (3.5 L)

100TH ANNIVERSARY
BOOK CREDITS

Beltrami Studios
Bob's Camera & Video
Erik Burkholder
Jeff Danziger
Leslie Dixon Photography
Amanda Lynn Douglas
Michael Austin Douglas
Helena Lelia Dunbar
Howard Francis Emerson
Eugene Philibert Galfetti
Harriet Waugh Galfetti
Kristen Peace Galfetti
Michael Anthony Galfetti
Stefan Hard Photography
Justin Tanner Jerome
Michael John Lavigne Sr.
Judy D'Amico May
John Miller, Sign Design

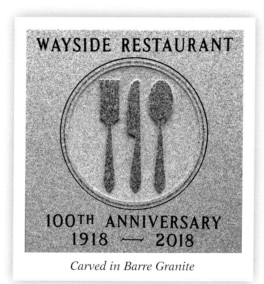

Carved in Barre Granite

Charlotte Jean Mitchell
Donald Roger Ordway
Douglas Allen Ordway
Jo-Ann Murielle Ordway
Suzanne Marie Potter
Edward Rubin Photography
Skip the Woodchuck
Karla Galfetti Smith
William Raymond Smith II
Randy Jay Spaulding
Floy Albra Virge
Jeff Raymond Virge
Jeff Raymond Virge II
Kevin Allen Virge
Brian Jay Zecchinelli
Jay Paul Zecchinelli
Karen Galfetti Zecchinelli
Nicholas Elgio Zecchinelli

RESTAURANT   BAKERY & CREAMERY

Contact us:
Wayside Restaurant, Bakery & Creamery
1873 U.S. Route 302
Montpelier, Vermont 05602
Phone: 802-223-6611
Email: eat@waysiderestaurant.com
Website: waysiderestaurant.com

ISBN: 978-0-87197-645-1
Library of Congress Control Number: 2017936677
Printed in China
10 9 8 7 6 5 4 3 2 1

Historic Hospitality Books

*It's Worth the Ride to the Wayside: Celebrating 100 Years
with Anniversary Ale, Yankee Cooking, and Ice Cream!*
was published by Historic Hospitality Books in
collaboration with the Wayside Restaurant, Bakery &
Creamery. Historic Hospitality Books creates exquisitely
designed custom books for America's iconic hotels, inns,
resorts, spas, and historic destinations. Historic Hospitality
Books is an imprint of Southwestern Publishing Group,
Inc., 2451 Atrium Way, Nashville, Tennessee 37214.
Southwestern Publishing Group is a wholly owned
subsidiary of Southwestern/Great American, Inc.,
Nashville, Tennessee.

Christopher G. Capen, President,
    Southwestern Publishing Group, Inc.
Sheila Thomas, Publisher, Historic Hospitality Books
Steve Newman, Cover and Layout Designer
Linda Brock, Project Manager and Editor
Kristin Connelly, Managing Editor
www.swpublishinggroup.com | 800-358-0560